to S

D0512704

The Calvary Road

by

Roy Hession

Much Love in Him

from
Val x

Rickfords Hill Publishing Ltd.

Published by

RICKFORDS HILL PUBLISHING LTD.

P.O. Box 576, Aylesbury, HP22 6XX, UK.

www.rhpbooks.co.uk

First published 1950
This edition 2010

ISBN 978-1-905044-27-6

Printed in Great Britain by Clays Ltd., St Ives plc.

Contents

Preface

This little book was first published some twenty-seven years ago. With the passage of years I am more sure now than even then that the truths expressed in these pages lie at the heart of all those movements of revival by which God has restored His church to new life in the hours of her dryness and need. Such movements of revival are not only glorious memories of the past, but are taking place right now in various parts of the world. The outward forms of such revivals do, of course, differ considerably but the inward and permanent content of them all is always the same—a new experience of conviction of sin among the saints; a new vision of the Cross of Jesus and of redemption; a new willingness on man's part for brokenness, repentance, confession and restitution; a joyful experience of the power of the blood of Jesus to cleanse fully from sin and restore and heal all that that sin has lost and broken; a new entering into the fulness of the Holy Spirit and of His power to do His own work through His people; and a new gathering in of the lost ones to Jesus. Inasmuch as this is just what is happening now in various parts of the world, these pages have a special relevance for the reader today and I trust may by the blessing of God be the means of helping many another to come to the Cross and present himself as a candidate for revival by the confession of his emptiness and failure. For revival is not a green valley getting greener, but a valley full of dry bones being made to live again and for those dead bones to stand up an exceeding great army (Ezek. 37). It is not good Christians becoming better Christians: as God sees us there are not any good Christians but rather Christians honestly confessing that their Christian life is a valley of dry bones and by that very confession qualifying for the grace that flows from the Cross and that makes all things new.

This little book expresses the truths that lie at the heart of revival just because it is itself the product of revival. As long ago as 1930 God began to work in a new way in the infant Church in Rwanda, East Africa. Infant that it was, it carried the seeds of decay within it, but a decay which God began to change into glorious fruitage when revival came. In the years that followed, the blessing of revival spread to the churches in the neighbouring countries of Uganda, Kenya and Tanzania. A great multitude of Africans, and missionaries among them, not only came to know Christ as their personal Saviour, but began to live a quality of life rarely experienced in even the most evangelical churches of the West. That movement of revival has continued in East Africa to the present day, if not in one part then in another, with all the vicissitudes and battles that one would naturally expect of a movement of life.

In 1947 I had been doing full-time evangelistic work in Great Britain for a number of years, but had come into a state of great spiritual need. I had somehow lost the power of the Holy Spirit which I once had known in the work of the Lord and yet I had to continue to conduct evangelistic campaigns without His power—a terrible experience! I was rather like that son of the prophets in Elisha's school who lost his axe-head while chopping down a tree, but who perhaps for a few strokes at least continued to chop with just the handle and wondered why he was making no progress with his work! Ignorant of what had really happened I redoubled my efforts and became increasingly tense and forceful, all of which was a poor substitute for the Spirit's gentle penetrating power. It is, of course, in looking back that I can describe my situation in this way. At the time I was all too ignorant of my need.

In April 1947 I invited several missionaries from East Africa to come as speakers to an Easter Conference which I was organising because I had heard that they had been experiencing revival in their field for a number of years and as an evangelist I was interested in revival. What they had to say was different from much of what I had associated with that word. It was very simple and very quiet. As they unfolded their message and gave their testimonies, I discovered that I was the neediest person in the Conference, and was far more in need of being revived than I had ever realised. That discovery, however, came only slowly to me. Being myself one of the speakers, I suppose I was more concerned about others' needs than my own. As my wife and others humbled themselves before God and experienced the cleansing of the blood of Jesus, I found myself left somewhat high and dry—dry just because I was high. I was humbled by the simplicity of the message, or rather the simplicity of what I had to do to be revived and filled with the Spirit. When at the end of the conference others testified as to how Jesus had broken them at His Cross and filled their hearts to overflowing with His Spirit, I had no such testimony. It was only afterwards that I was enabled to give up trying to fit things into my doctrinal scheme and come humbly to the Cross for cleansing from my own personal sins. It was like beginning my Christian life all over again. My flesh 'came again like that of a little child', as did Naaman's when he was willing to humble himself and dip himself in Jordan. It has been an altogether new chapter in life since then. It has meant, however, that I have had to choose constantly to die to the big 'I', that Jesus might be all, and constantly to come to Him for cleansing in His precious blood. But that is why it is a new chapter.

The things learned at that time and in the months that followed were committed to paper and were published mostly as articles, later to be collected together to form this book. In the years that have followed its publication, its distribution has spread throughout the whole English-speaking world and has been translated into some forty languages—to the astonishment of no one more than the one who penned it. Its wide dissemination is simply the evidence of the hunger of Christians throughout the world for reality and a Christianity that really works. More than that, it is one of many evidences that 'the time to favour Zion, even the set time has come' (Ps. 102:13) and that God's purpose to build again 'the walls of Jerusalem that are broken down' is coming to pass.

It must not be thought that this book represents a purely personal contribution on my part. The things recorded in this book have been learned in fellowship with others in various parts who have begun to walk the way of the Cross in a new way. Any one of a number in that fellowship might have written these chapters equally well. It is a fellowship, too, that is continually growing, for an ever increasing number of lives have been greatly influenced right across the world, as teams have gone to this and that country and numerous tours undertaken. This fact, I think, adds to the strength and significance of what is here written. One realises, of course, that this stream of blessing of which one has been a part is but one of a number of streams of new life, all of which emanate from the same source of the Cross and are contributing to the deeply needed revival of the church.

Leaving the mountain, the streamlet grows,
Flooding the vale with a river;
So, from the hill of the Cross, there flows
Life more abundant for ever.

Over the years some have occasionally queried the use of the term revival to describe the sort of message and experience expressed in this book, pointing to the fact that they cannot see any spectacular religious awakening, involving great numbers of people, with many turning to the Lord, such as is popularly associated with the word revival. Somehow we have never been able to accede to this objection. Rather we would doggedly insist that the things we have been learning over these years, some of which are written in these chapters, are the very essence of revival and would, if widely responded to and deeply applied, result indeed in the widest revival of the church— as wide as the response to the call to brokenness at the Cross is wide. Certainly for those who have humbled themselves under the hand of God at that place where sins are washed away, it has meant the revival of their Christian lives in the truest and simplest sense of the word. There are indeed now ever expanding beach heads of revival in many hearts, in many fellowships and many churches and in various lands. It is for those in whose hearts Jesus has established such beach-heads to hold fast the vision that that which they have discovered and are continually discovering in experience is revival indeed and to know that God's establishment of such beach-heads is surely but the prelude for His invasion in mighty and wide-ranging power into our situations of need. As I write heartening news comes that His invasions in power are in fact occurring in this and that place and God is reviving His church in this wider way according to His sovereign grace. May we be willing in this the day of His power!

This leads me to say a word about the necessary attitude of heart for the reader. If God is to bless him at all through these pages he must come to them with a deep hunger of heart. He must be possessed with a dissatisfaction of the state of the church in general, and of himself in particular—especially of himself. He must be willing for God to begin His work in himself first, rather than in the other man. He must, moreover, be possessed with the holy expectancy that God can and will meet his need. If he is in any sense a Christian leader, the urgency of the matter is intensified many times over. His willingness to admit his need and be blessed will determine the degree to which God can bless the people to whom he ministers. Above all, he must realise that he must be the first to humble himself at the Cross. If a new honesty with regard to sin is needed among his people, he must begin with himself. It was when the King of Nineveh arose from his throne, covered himself with sack cloth and sat in ashes as a sign of his repentance that his people repented.

Let not, however, those readers who are not leaders be tempted to look at those who are and wait for them. God wants to begin with each one of us. He wants to begin with YOU.

Just one more thing needs to be said here about this book. Owing to the fact that these chapters first appeared as articles in a little publication my wife and I were issuing, and inasmuch as we tried to make each article complete in itself, it will be found, now that they are put together, that there is a good deal of over-lapping, and certain things will be seen to be repeated again and again. It cannot, therefore, be regarded as an ordinary book and the chapters might best be read each one on its own rather than the whole of them at one sitting.

May God bless us all.

Roy Hession
November 1977

1

Brokenness

We want to be very simple in this matter of revival. Revival is just the life of the Lord Jesus poured into human hearts. Jesus is always victorious. In heaven they are praising Him all the time for His victory. Whatever may be our experience of failure and barrenness, He is never defeated. His power is boundless. We, on our part, have only to get into a right relationship with Him, and we shall see His power being demonstrated in our hearts and lives and service, and His victorious life will fill us and overflow through us to others. That is revival in its essence.

If, however, we are to come into this right relationship with Him, the first thing we must learn is that our wills must be broken to His will. To be broken is the beginning of revival. It is painful, it is humiliating, but it is the only way. It is being 'Not I, but Christ',[1] and a 'C' is a bent 'I'. The Lord Jesus cannot live in us fully and reveal Himself through us until the proud self within us is broken. This simply means that the hard, unyielding self, which justifies itself, wants its own way, stands up for its rights, and seeks its own glory, at last bows its head to God's will, admits

---
[1] Gal. 2:20

its wrong, gives up its own way to Jesus, surrenders its rights, and discards its own glory—that the Lord Jesus might have all and be all. In other words, it is dying to self and self-attitudes.

As we look honestly at our Christian lives, we can see how much of this self there is in each of us. It is so often self who tries to live the Christian life (the mere fact that we use the word 'try' indicates that it is self who has the responsibility). It is self, too, who is often doing Christian work. It is always self who gets irritable, envious, resentful, critical, and worried. It is self who is hard and unyielding in its attitudes to others. It is self who is shy, self-conscious, and reserved. No wonder we need breaking. As long as self is in control, God can do little with us, for the fruit of the Spirit (enumerated in Gal. 5), with which God longs to fill us, is the complete antithesis of the hard, unbroken spirit within us and presupposes that self has been crucified.

Being broken is both God's work and ours. He brings His pressure to bear, but we have to make the choice. If we are really open to conviction as we seek fellowship with God (and willingness for the light is the prime condition of fellowship with God), God will show us the expressions of this proud, hard self that cause Him pain. Then it is, we can stiffen our necks and refuse to repent, or we can bow the head and say, 'Yes, Lord.' Brokenness in daily experience is simply the response of humility to the conviction of God, and inasmuch as this conviction is continuous, we shall need to be broken continually. This can be very costly, when we see all the yielding of rights and selfish interests that this will involve, and the confessions and restitutions that sometimes may be necessary.

For this reason, we are not likely to be broken except at the Cross of Jesus. The willingness of Jesus to be broken for us is the all-compelling motive in our being broken too. We see Him, who is in the form of God, counting not equality with God a prize to be grasped at and hung on to, but letting it go for us and taking upon Him the form of a Servant—God's Servant, man's Servant. We see Him willing to have no rights of His own, no home of His own, no possessions of His own, willing to let men revile Him and not revile again, willing to let men tread on Him and not retaliate or defend Himself. Above all, we see Him broken as He meekly goes to Calvary to become men's scapegoat by bearing their sins in His own body on the Tree. In a pathetic passage in a prophetic Psalm, He says, 'I am a worm, and no man' (Psalm 22:6). Those who have been in tropical lands tell us that there is a big difference between a snake and a worm when you attempt to strike at them. The snake rears itself up, hisses, and tries to strike back—a true picture of self. But a worm offers no resistance, it allows you to do what you like with it, kick it or squash it under your heel—a picture of true brokenness. Jesus was willing to become just that for us—a worm and no man; and He did so, because that is what He saw us to be, worms having forfeited all rights by our sin, except to deserve hell. He now calls us to take our rightful place as worms for Him and with Him. The whole Sermon on the Mount, with its teaching of non-retaliation, love for enemies, and selfless giving, assumes that that is our position. But only the vision of the Love that was willing to be broken for us can constrain us to be willing for that.

> Lord, bend that proud and stiff-necked I,
> Help me to bow the head and die;
> Beholding Him on Calvary,
> Who bowed His head for me.

But dying to self is not a thing we do once for all. There may be an initial dying when God first shows these things, but ever after, it will be a constant dying, for only so can the Lord Jesus be revealed constantly through us (2 Cor. 4:10). All day long the choice will be before us in a thousand ways. It will mean no plans, no time, no money, no pleasure of our own. It will mean a constant yielding to those around us, for our yieldedness to God is measured by our yieldedness to man. Every humiliation, everyone who tries and vexes us, is God's way of breaking us, so that there is a yet deeper channel in us for the Life of Christ.

You see, the only life that pleases God, and that can be victorious, is His life—never our life, no matter how hard we try. But inasmuch as our self-centred life is the exact opposite of His, we can never be filled with His life, unless we are prepared for God to bring our life constantly to death. And in that we must co-operate by our moral choice.

2

Cups Running Over

Brokenness, however, is but the beginning of revival. Revival itself is being absolutely filled to overflowing with the Holy Spirit, and that is victorious living. If we were asked this moment if we were filled with the Holy Spirit, how many of us would dare to answer 'Yes'? Revival is when we can say 'yes' at any moment of the day. It is not egoistic to say so, for filling to overflowing is utterly and completely God's work—it is all of grace. All we have to do is to present our empty, broken self and let Him fill and keep filled. Andrew Murray says, 'Just as water ever seeks and fills the lowest place, so the moment God finds you abased and empty, His glory and power flow in.' The picture that has made things simple and clear to so many of us is that of the human heart as a cup which we hold out to Jesus, longing that he may fill it with the Water of Life. Jesus is pictured as bearing the golden water-pot with the Water of Life. As He passes by, He looks into our cup, and if it is clean He fills it to overflowing with the Water of Life; and as Jesus is always passing by, the cup can be always running over. That is something of what David meant when he said, 'My cup runneth over.' This is revival—the constant peace of God ruling in our hearts because we are full to overflowing with blessing ourselves, and sharing it with others. People imagine that dying to self makes one miserable, but it is just the opposite. It is the refusal to die to self that makes one miserable. The more we know of death with Him, the more we shall know of His life in us, and so the more of real peace and joy. His life, too, will overflow through us to lost souls in a real concern for their salvation, and to our fellow Christians in a deep desire for their blessing.

Under the Blood

Only one thing prevents Jesus filling our cups as He passes by, and that is sin in one of its thousand forms. The Lord Jesus does not fill dirty cups. Anything that springs from self, however small it may be, is sin. Self-effort or self-complacency in service is sin. Self-pity in trials or difficulties, self-seeking in business or Christian work, self-indulgence in one's spare time, sensitiveness, touchiness, resentment, and self-defence when we are hurt or injured by others, self-consciousness, reserve, worry, fear, all spring from self and all are sin and make our cups unclean.'[2] But all of them were put into that other

[2] Some may be inclined to question whether it is right to call such things as self-consciousness, reserve, and fear, sins. 'Call them infirmities, disabilities, temperamental weaknesses, if you will,' some have said, 'but not sins. To do so would be to get us into bondage.' The reverse, however, is true. If these things are not sins, then we must put up with them for the rest of our lives, there is no deliverance. But if these and other things like them are indeed sins, then there is a Fountain for sin, and we may experience cleansing and deliverance from them, if we put them immediately 'under His precious Blood' the moment we are conscious of them. And they are sins. Their source is unbelief and an inverted form of pride, and they have hindered and hidden Him times without number.

cup, which the Lord Jesus shrank from momentarily in Gethsemane, but which he drank to the dregs at Calvary— the cup of our sin; and if we will allow Him to show us what is in our cups and then give it Him, He will cleanse them in the precious Blood that still flows for sin. That does not mean mere cleansing from the guilt of sin, but from the stain and pollution of it, so that we have 'no more conscience of sin' there. And as He cleanses our cups, so He fills them to overflowing with His Holy Spirit.

And we are able daily to avail ourselves of that precious Blood. Suppose you have let the Lord Jesus cleanse your cup and have trusted Him to fill it to overflowing, then something comes along—a touch of envy or temper. What happens? Your cup becomes dirty and it ceases to overflow; and if we are constantly being defeated in this way, then our cup is never overflowing.

If we are to know continuous revival we must learn the way to keep our cups clean. It is never God's will that a revival should cease and be known in history as the revival of this or that year. When that happens it is due to one thing only—sin, just those little sins that the devil drops into our cup. But if we will go back to Calvary and learn afresh the power of the Blood of Jesus to cleanse moment by moment from the beginnings of sin, then we have learnt the secret of cups constantly cleansed and constantly overflowing. The moment you are conscious of that touch of envy, criticism, irritability, whatever it is—give it to Jesus and ask Him to cleanse it away by the power of His Blood, and you will find the reaction gone, your joy and peace restored, and your cup running over; and the more you come for cleansing in this way, the less even will you have these reactions. But cleansing is possible only when we have first been broken before God on the point concerned. Suppose we are irritated by certain traits in someone. It is not enough just to take our reactions of irritation to Calvary. We must first be broken, that is, we must yield to God over the whole question, and accept that person and their ways as His Will for us. Then we are able to take our wrong reaction to Jesus, knowing that His Blood will cleanse away our sin. When we have been cleansed from sin, let us not keep mourning over it; let us not be occupied with ourselves, but let us look up to our victorious Lord, and praise Him that He is still victorious.

There is one simple but all-inclusive guide the Word of God gives to regulate our walk with Jesus and to make us to know when sin has come in. Col. 3:15 says, 'Let the peace of God rule in your hearts.' Everything that disturbs the peace of God in our hearts is sin, no matter how small it is, and no matter how little like sin it may at first appear to be.

This peace is to 'rule' our hearts, or (a more literal translation) 'be the referee' in our hearts. When the referee blows his whistle at a football match the game has to stop, a foul has been committed. When we lose our peace, God's referee in our hearts has blown his whistle! Let us stop immediately, ask God to show us what is wrong, confess to Him the sin He shows us, and then peace will be restored by the Blood of Jesus, and we shall go on our way with our cups running over. If, however, God does not give us His peace, it will be because we are not really broken. Perhaps we have yet to say 'Sorry' to somebody else as well as to God. Or perhaps we still feel it is the other person's fault. But if we have lost our peace, it is obvious whose fault it is. We do not lose peace with God over another person's sin, but only over our own. God wants to show us our reactions, and only when we are willing to be cleansed there will we have His peace. Oh, what a simple but searching thing it is to be ruled by the peace of God, none other than the Holy Spirit Himself! Former selfish ways, which we never bothered about, are now shown to us, and we cannot walk in them without the referee blowing his whistle. Grumbling, bossiness, carelessness, down to the smallest thing are all revealed as sins when we are prepared to let our days be ruled by the peace of God. Many times a day, and over the smallest things, we shall have to avail ourselves of the cleansing Blood of Jesus, and we shall find ourselves walking the way of brokenness as never before. But Jesus will be manifested in all His loveliness and grace in that brokenness.

Many of us, however, have neglected the referee's whistle so often and for so long that we have ceased to hear it. Days follow days, and we feel we have little need of cleansing and no occasion of being broken. In that condition we are usually in a worse state than we ever imagine. It will need a great hunger for restored fellowship with God to possess our hearts before we will be willing to cry to God to show us where the Blood of Jesus must be applied. He will show us, to begin with, just one thing, and it will be our obedience and brokenness on that one thing that will be the first step into revival for us.

3

The Way of Fellowship

When man fell and chose to make himself, rather than God, the centre of his life, the effect was not only to put man out of fellowship with God, but also out of fellowship with his fellow man. The story of man's first quarrel with God in the third chapter of Genesis is closely followed in the fourth chapter by the story of man's first quarrel with his fellow, Cain's murder of Abel. The Fall is simply, 'we have turned every one to his own way'.[3] If I want my own way rather than God's, it is quite obvious that I shall want my own way rather than the other man's. A man does not assert his independence of God to surrender it to a fellow man, if he can help it. But a world in which each man wants his own way cannot but be a world full of tensions, barriers, suspicions, misunderstandings, clashes and conflicts.

Now the work of the Lord Jesus Christ on the Cross was not only to bring men back into fellowship with God, but also into fellowship with their fellow men. Indeed, it cannot do one without the other. As the spokes get nearer the centre of the wheel, they get nearer to one another. If, however, we have not been brought into vital fellowship

[3] Is. 53:6

with our brother, it is a proof that to that extent we have not been brought into vital fellowship with God. The first epistle of John (what a new light revival sheds on this Scripture!) insists on testing the depth and reality of a man's fellowship with God by the depth and reality of his fellowship with his brethren.[4] Some of us have come to see how utterly connected a man's relationship to his fellows is with his relationship to God. Everything that comes as a barrier between us and another, be it never so small, comes as a barrier between us and God. We have found that where these barriers are not put right immediately, they get thicker and thicker until we find ourselves shut off from God and our brother by what seem to be veritable brick walls. Quite obviously, if we allow new life to come to us, it will have to manifest itself by a walk of oneness with God and our brother, with nothing between.

Light and Darkness

On what basis can we have real fellowship with God and our brother? Here 1 John 1:7 has come afresh to us. 'If we walk in the light, as he is in the light, we have fellowship one with another, and the Blood of Jesus Christ his Son cleanseth us from all sin.' What is meant by light and darkness is that light reveals, darkness hides. When anything reproves us, shows us up as we really are—that is light. 'Whatsoever doth make manifest is light.'[5] But whenever we do anything or say anything (or do not say anything) to hide what we are or what we've done—that is darkness.

Now the first effect of sin in our lives is always to make

---

[4] 1 John 2:9; 3:14-15; 4:20   [5] Eph. 5:13

us try to hide what we are. Sin made our first parents hide behind the trees of the garden, and it has had the same effect on us ever since. Sin always involves us in being unreal, pretending, duplicity, window dressing, excusing ourselves and blaming others—and we can do all that as much by our silence as by saying or doing something. This is what the previous verse calls 'walking in darkness'. With some of us, the sin in question may be nothing more than self-consciousness (anything with 'I' in it is sin) and the hiding, nothing more than an assumed heartiness to cover that self-consciousness, but it is walking in darkness none the less.

In contrast to all this in us, verse 5 of this chapter tells us that 'God is light', that is, God is the All-revealing One who shows up every man as he really is. It goes on to say, 'in him is no darkness at all', that is, there is absolutely nothing in God which can be one with the tiniest bit of darkness or hiding in us.

Quite obviously, then, it is utterly impossible for us to be walking in any degree of darkness and have fellowship with God. While we are in that condition of darkness, we cannot have true fellowship with our brother either—for we are not real with him, and no one can have fellowship with an unreal person. A wall of reserve separates him and us.

The Only Basis for Fellowship

The only basis for real fellowship with God and man is to live out in the open with both. 'But if we walk in the light, as he is in the light, we have fellowship one with another.' To walk in the light is the opposite of walking in darkness. Spurgeon defines it in one of his sermons as 'the willingness to know and be known'. As far as God is concerned, this means that we are willing to know the whole truth about ourselves, we are open to conviction. We will bend the neck to the first twinges of conscience. Everything He shows us to be sin we will deal with as sin—we will hide or excuse nothing. Such a walk in the light cannot but discover sin increasingly in our lives, and we shall see things to be sin which we never thought to be such before. For that reason we might shrink from this walk, and be tempted to make for cover. But the verse goes on with the precious words, 'and the Blood of Jesus Christ his Son cleanseth us from all sin.' Everything that the light of God shows up as sin we can confess and carry to the Fountain of Blood, and it is gone, gone from God's sight and gone from our hearts. By the power of the precious Blood we can be made more stainless than the driven snow; and thus continually abiding in the light and cleansed by the Blood, we have fellowship with God.

The fellowship promised us here, however, is not only with God, but 'one with another', and that involves us in walking in the light with our brother too. In any case we cannot be 'in the open' with God, and 'in the dark' with him. This means that we must be as willing to know the truth about ourselves from our brother as to know it from God. We must be prepared for him to hold the light to us (and we must be willing to do the same service for him) and challenge us in love about anything he sees in our lives which is not the highest. We must be willing not only to know, but also to be known by him for what we really are. That means we are not going to hide our inner selves from those with whom we ought to be in fellowship; we are not going to window dress and put on appearances; nor are we going to whitewash and excuse ourselves. We are going to be honest about ourselves with them. We are willing to give up our spiritual privacy, pocket our pride, and risk our reputations for the sake of being open and transparent with our brethren in Christ. It means, too, that we are not going to cherish any wrong feeling in our hearts about another, but we are first going to claim deliverance from it from God and put it right with the one concerned. As we walk this way, we shall find that we shall have fellowship with one another at an altogether new level, and we shall not love one another less, but infinitely more.

No Bondage

Walking in the light is simply walking with Jesus. Therefore, there need be no bondage about it. We have not necessarily got to tell everybody everything about ourselves. The fundamental thing is our attitude of walking in the light, rather than the act. Are we willing to be in the open with our brother—and be so in word when God tells us to? That is the 'armour of light'—true transparency. This may sometimes be humbling, but it will help us to a new reality with Christ, and to a new self-knowledge. We have become so used to the fact that God knows all about us that it does not seem to register with us, and we inevitably end by not knowing the truth about ourselves. But let a man begin to be absolutely honest about himself with but one other, as God guides him, and he will come to a knowledge of himself and his sins that he never had before, and he will begin to see more clearly than ever before where the redemption of Christ has got to be applied progressively to his life. This is the reason why James tells us to put ourselves under the discipline of 'confessing our faults one to another'.

In 1 John 1:7, of course, the purpose of 'walking in the light' is that we might 'have fellowship one with another'. And what fellowship it is when we walk this way together! Obviously, love will flow from one to another when each is prepared to be known as the repentant sinner he is at the Cross of Jesus. When the barriers are down and the masks are off, God has a chance of making us really one. But there is also the added joy of knowing that in such a fellowship we are 'safe'. No fear now that others may be thinking thoughts about us or having reactions toward us, which they are hiding from us. In a fellowship which is committed to walk in the light beneath the Cross, we know that if there is any thought about us, it will quickly be brought into the light, either in brokenness and confession (where there has been wrong and unlove), or else as a loving challenge, as something that we ought to know about ourselves.

It must not, however, be forgotten that our walk in the light is first and foremost with the Lord Jesus. It is with Him first that we must get things settled, and it is His cleansing and victory that must first be obtained. Then when God guides us to open our hearts with others, we come to them with far more of a testimony than a confession (except where that is specifically due), and we praise God together.

Teams of Two for Revival

Jesus wants you to begin walking in the light with Him in a new way today. Join with one other—your Christian friend, the person you live with, your wife, your husband.

Drop the mask. God has doubtless convicted you of one thing more than another that you have got to be honest with them about. Start there. Be a team of two to work for revival amongst your circle. As others are broken at the Cross they will be added to your fellowship, as God leads. Get together from time to time for fellowship and to share your spiritual experience with real openness. In complete oneness pray together for others, and go out as a team with fresh testimony. God, through such a fellowship, will begin to work wondrously. As He saves and blesses others in this vital way, they can start to live and work as a fellowship too. As one billiard ball will move another billiard ball, so one group will set off another group, until the whole of our land is covered with new life from the risen Lord Jesus.

4

The Highway of Holiness

One of the things that we must learn if we are to live the victorious Christian life is its utter simplicity. How complicated we have made it! Great volumes are written; all sorts of technical phrases are used; we are told the secret lies in this, or that, and so on. But to most of us, it is all so complicated that, although we know it in theory, we are unable to relate what we know to our practical daily living. In order to make the simplest truths we have been considering even clearer, we want in this chapter to cast them all in picture form.

The Highway

An 'overall' picture of the life of victory, which has come to many of us, is that of the Highway in Isa. 35: 'And an highway shall be there, and a way, and it shall be called The way of holiness.' The picture is that of a Highway built up from the surrounding morass, the world. Though the Highway is narrow and uphill, it is not beyond any of us to walk it, for 'the wayfaring men, though fools, shall not err therein.' Though there are many dangers if we get off the road, while we keep to the Highway there is safety, for 'no lion shall be there, nor any ravenous beast shall go up thereon.' Only one kind of person is barred from walking there, and that is the unclean one. 'The unclean shall not pass over it.' This includes not only the sinner who does not know Christ as his Saviour, but also the Christian who does, and yet is walking in unconfessed and uncleansed sin.

The only way on to the Highway is up a small, dark, forbidding hill—the Hill of Calvary. It is the sort of hill we have to climb on our hands and knees—especially our knees. If we are content with our present Christian life, if we do not desire with a desperate hunger to get on to the Highway, we shall never get to our knees, and thus never climb the hill. But if we are dissatisfied, if we are hungry, then we will find ourselves ascending. Do not hurry. Let God make you really hungry for the Highway; let Him really drive you to your knees in longing prayer. Mere sightseers won't get very far. 'Ye shall seek me, and find me, when ye shall search for me with all your heart.'[6]

A Low Door

At the top of the hill, guarding the way to the Highway, stands so gaunt and grim... the Cross. There it stands, the Divider of time and the Divider of men. At the foot of the Cross is a low door, so low that to get through it one has to stoop and crawl through. It is the only entrance to the Highway. We must go through it if we would go any farther on our way. This door is called the Door of the Broken Ones. Only the broken can enter the Highway. To be broken means to be 'not I, but Christ'. There is in every one of us a proud stiff-necked 'I'. The stiff neck began in

[6] Jer. 29:13

the garden of Eden when Adam and Eve, who had always bowed their heads in surrender to God's will, stiffened their necks, struck out for independence, and tried to be 'as gods'. All the way through the Bible God charges His people with the same stiff neck; and it manifests itself in us, too. We are hard and unyielding. We are sensitive and easily hurt. We get irritable, envious, and critical. We are resentful and unforgiving. We strive in our own strength and attempt to do by our own efforts what should be left to God. We are self-indulgent—and how often that can lead to impurity! Every one of these things, and many more, spring from this proud self within. If it were not there and Christ were in its place, we would not have these reactions. Before we can enter the Highway, God must bend and break that stiff-necked self, so that Christ reigns in its stead. To be broken means to have no rights before God and man. It does not mean merely surrendering my rights to Him, but rather recognizing that I haven't any, except to deserve hell. It means just being nothing and having nothing that I call my own, neither time, money, possessions, nor position.

In order to break our wills to His, God brings us to the foot of the Cross and there shows us what real brokenness is. We see those wounded Hands and Feet, that Face of Love crowned with thorns, and we see, the complete brokenness of the One who said, 'Not my will, but Thine be done',[7] as He drank the bitter cup of our sin to its dregs. So the way to be broken is to look on Him and to realize it was our sin which nailed Him there. Then as we see the love and brokenness of the God who died in our place, our

---

[7] Luke 22:42

hearts will become strangely melted and we will want to be broken for Him, and we shall pray,

> Oh, to be saved from myself, dear Lord,
> Oh, to be lost in Thee,
> Oh, that it might be no more I,
> But Christ that lives in me.

Some of us have found that there is no prayer that God is so swift to answer as the prayer that He might break us.

A Constant Choice

Do not let us imagine, however, that we have to be broken only once as we go through the door. Ever after it will be a constant choice before us. God brings His pressure to bear on us, but we have to make the choice. If someone hurts and slights us, we immediately have the choice of accepting the slight as a means of grace to humble us lower, or we can resist it and stiffen our necks again with all the disturbance of spirit that that is bound to bring. Right the way through the day our brokenness will be tested, and it is no use our pretending we are broken before God if we are not broken in our attitude to those around us. God nearly always tests us through other people. There are no second causes for the Christian. God's will is made known in His providences, and His providences are so often others with their many demands on us. If you find yourself in a patch of unbrokenness, the only way is to go afresh to Calvary and see Christ broken for you, and you will come away willing to be broken for Him.

Over the Door of the Broken Ones is sprinkled the precious Blood of the Lord Jesus. As we bend to crawl through, the Blood cleanses from all sin, for not only have we to bend to get through, but only the clean can walk the Highway. Maybe you have never known Jesus as your Saviour; maybe you have known Him for years; but in either case you are defiled by sin, the sins of pride, envy, resentment, impurity, etc. If you will give them all to Him who bore them on the Cross, He will whisper to you again what He once said on the Cross, 'It is finished', and your heart will be cleansed whiter than snow.

The Gift of His Fullness

So we get on to the Highway. There it stretches before us, a narrow, uphill road, bathed in light, leading towards the Heavenly Jerusalem. The embankment on either side slopes away into thick darkness. In fact, the darkness creeps right to the very edges of the Highway, but on the Highway itself all is light. Behind us is the Cross, no longer dark and forbidding, but radiant and glowing, and we no longer see Jesus stretched across its arms, but walking the Highway overflowing with resurrection life. In His Hands He carries a pitcher with the Water of Life. He comes right up to us and asks us to hold out our hearts, and just as if we were handing Him a cup, we present to Him our empty hearts. He looks inside—a painful scrutiny—and where He sees we have allowed His Blood to cleanse them, He fills them with the Water of Life. So we go on our way rejoicing and praising God and overflowing with His new life. This is revival, you and I full of the Holy Spirit all the time, loving others and concerned for their salvation. No struggling, no tarrying; just simply giving Him each sin to cleanse in His precious Blood and accepting from His hands the free gift of His Fullness, and then allowing Him to do the work through us. As we walk along with Him, He is always there continually filling so that our cups continually overflow.

So the rest of our Christian life simply consists now of walking along the Highway, with hearts overflowing, bowing the neck to His will all the time, constantly trusting the Blood to cleanse us, and living in complete oneness with Jesus. There is nothing spectacular about this life, no emotional experiences to sigh after and wait for. It is just plain day—today living of the life the Lord intended us to live. This is real holiness.

Off the Highway

But we may, and sometimes do, slip off the Highway, for it is narrow. One little step aside and we are off the path and in darkness. It is always because of a failure in obedience somewhere or a failure to be weak enough to let God do all. Satan is always beside the road, shouting at us, but he cannot touch us. But we can yield to his voice by an act of will. This is the beginning of sin and slipping away from Jesus. Sometimes we find ourselves stiffening our necks to someone, sometimes to God Himself. Sometimes jealousy or resentment assails us. Sometimes we find ourselves tense and striving, without resting in Him. Immediately we are over the side, for nothing unclean can walk the Highway. Our cup is dirtied and ceases to overflow, and we lose our peace with God. If we do not come back to the Highway at once, we shall go farther down the side. We must get back. How? The first thing to do is to ask God to show what caused us to slip off; and He will, though it often takes Him time to make us see. Perhaps someone annoyed me, and I was irritated. God wants me to see that it was not the thing that the person did that matters, but my reaction to it. If I had been broken, I would not have been irritated. So, as I look longingly back to the Highway, I see the Lord Jesus again, and I see what an ugly thing it is to get irritable, and that Jesus died to save me from being irritable. As I crawl up again to the Highway on hands and knees, I come again to Him and His Blood for cleansing. Jesus is waiting there to fill my cup to overflowing once again. Hallelujah! No matter where you leave the Highway, you will always find Him calling you to come back and be broken again, and always the Blood will be there to cleanse and make you clean. This is the great secret of the Highway—knowing what to do with sin, when sin has come in. The secret is always to take sin to the Cross, see there its sinfulness, confess it to God, and reckon it gone, through the value of the Blood of Jesus.

So the real test all along the Highway will be—are our cups running over? Have we the peace of God in our hearts? Have we love and concern for others? These things are the barometer of the Highway. If they are disturbed, then sin has crept in somewhere—self-pity, self-seeking, self-indulgence in thought or deed, sensitiveness, touchiness, self-defence, striving in our own strength, self-consciousness, shyness, reserve, worry, fear, and so on.

Our Walk with Others

An important thing about the Highway which has not been mentioned yet is that we do not walk this Highway alone. Others walk it with us. There is, of course, the Lord Jesus. But there are other wayfarers, too, and the rule of the road is that fellowship with them is as important as fellowship with Jesus. Indeed, the two are intimately connected. Our relationship with our fellows and our relationship with God are so linked that we cannot disturb one without disturbing the other. Everything that comes between us and another, such as impatience, resentment, or envy, comes between us and God. These barriers are sometimes no more than veils—veils through which we can still, to some extent, see. But if not removed immediately, they thicken into blankets and then into brick walls, and we are shut off from both God and our fellows, shut in to ourselves. It is clear why these two relationships should be so linked. 'God is love', that is love for others, and the moment we fail in love towards another, we put ourselves out of fellowship with God—for God loves him, even if we do not.

But more than that, the effect of such sins is always to make us 'walk in darkness'[8]—that is, to cover it up and hide what we really are or what we are really feeling. That is always the meaning of 'darkness' in Scripture, for while the light reveals, the darkness hides. The first effect of sin in us is always to make us hide, with the result that we are pretending, we are wearing a mask, we are not real with either God or man. And, of course, neither God nor man can have fellowship with an unreal person.

The way back into fellowship with the Lord Jesus will bring us again into fellowship with our brother, too. All unlove must be recognized as sin and confessed as such that it may be covered by the Blood of Jesus—and then it can be put right with our brother also. As we come back

---

[8] 1 John 2:9-11

to the Lord Jesus like this, we shall find His love for our brother filling our hearts and wanting to express itself in our actions toward him, and we shall walk in fellowship together again.

So this is the Highway life. It is no new, astounding doctrine. It is not something new for us to preach. It is quite unspectacular. It is just a life to live day by day in whatever circumstances the Lord has put us. It does not contradict what we may have read or heard about the Christian life. It just puts into simple pictorial language the great truths of sanctification. To start to live this life now will mean revival in our lives. To continue to live it will be revival continued. Revival is just you and I walking along the Highway in complete oneness with the Lord Jesus and with one another, with cups continually cleansed and overflowing with the life and love of God.

5

The Dove and the Lamb

Victorious living and effective soul-winning service are not the product of our better selves and hard endeavours, but are simply the fruit of the Holy Spirit. We are not called upon to produce the fruit, but simply to bear it. It is all the time to be His fruit. Nothing is more important, then, than that we should be continually filled with the Holy Spirit, or to keep to the metaphor, that the 'trees of the Lord should be continually full of sap'—His sap.

How this may be so for us is graphically illustrated by the record, in the first chapter of John, of how the Holy Spirit came upon the Lord Jesus at His baptism. John the Baptist had seen Jesus coming to him and had said of Him, 'Behold, the Lamb of God, which taketh away the sin of the world.' Then as he baptized Him, he saw the heavens opened and the Spirit of God descending like a Dove and lighting upon Him.

The Humility of God

What a suggestive picture we have here—the Dove descending upon the Lamb and resting upon Him! The Lamb and the Dove are surely the gentlest of all God's creatures. The Lamb speaks of meekness and submissiveness, and the Dove speaks of peace (what more peaceful sound than the cooing of a dove on a summer day). Does not this suggest that in the very heart of Deity there is humility? When the eternal God chose to reveal Himself in His Son, He gave Him the name of the Lamb; and when it was necessary for the Holy Spirit to come into the world He was revealed under the emblem of the Dove. Is it not obvious, then, that the reason why we have to be humble in order to walk with God is not merely because God is so big and we so little that humility befits such little creatures—but because God, as seen in Jesus, is meek and lowly in heart Himself?

The main lesson of this incident is that the Holy Spirit, as the Dove, could come upon and remain upon the Lord Jesus only because He was the Lamb. Had the Lord Jesus had any other disposition than that of the Lamb—humility, submissiveness, and self-surrender—the Dove could never have rested on Him. Being Himself so gentle, He would have been frightened away had not Jesus been meek and lowly in heart.

Here, then, we have pictured for us the condition upon which the same Holy Spirit can come upon us and abide upon us. The Dove can abide upon us only as we are willing to be as the Lamb. How impossible that He should rest upon us while self is unbroken! The manifestations of the unbroken self are the direct opposite of the gentleness of the Dove. Read again in Gal. 5 the ninefold fruit of the Spirit ('love, joy, peace, longsuffering, gentleness, goodness, faithfulness, meekness, self-control') with which the Dove longs to fill us! Then contrast it with the ugly works of the flesh (the New Testament name for the unbroken self) in the same chapter. It is the contrast of the snarling wolf with the gentle dove!

The Disposition of the Lamb[9]

How clear, then, that the Holy Spirit will come upon us and remain upon us only as we are willing to be as the Lamb on each point on which He will convict us! And nothing is so searching and humbling as to look at the Lamb on His way to Calvary for us and to be shown in how many points we have been unwilling to take the position of the lamb for Him.

Look at Him for a moment as the Lamb. He was the simple Lamb. A lamb is the simplest of God's creatures. It has no schemes or plans for helping itself—it exists in helplessness and simplicity. Jesus made Himself as nothing for us, and became the simple Lamb. He had no strength of His own or wisdom of His own, no schemes to get Himself out of difficulties, just simple dependence on the Father all the time. 'The Son can do nothing of himself, but what he seeth the Father do.' But we—how complicated we are! What schemes we have had of helping ourselves and of getting ourselves out of difficulties! What efforts of our own we have resorted to, to live the Christian life and to do God's works, as if we were something and could do something! The Dove had to take His flight (at least as far as the conscious blessing of His Presence was concerned) because we were not willing to be simple lambs.

Willing to be Shorn

Then He was the shorn Lamb, willing to be shorn of His

---

[9] I owe the succinct headings, under which the picture of The Lamb of God is given in these paragraphs, to an address I heard my friend, Marshall Shallis of England, give some five ago.

rights, His reputation, and every human liberty that was due to Him, just as a lamb is shorn of its wool. He never resisted. A lamb never does. When He was reviled for our sakes, He reviled not again. When He suffered, He threatened not. He never said, 'You cannot treat me like that. Don't you know that I am the Son of God?' But we— ah, we, on how many occasions have we been unwilling to be shorn of that which was our right. We were not willing for His sake to lose what was our own. We insisted, too, that we should be treated with the respect due to our position. We resisted, and we fought. The Dove had to take His flight from us, for we were not willing to be shorn lambs, and we were left without peace, hard and unloving.

He Answered Nothing

Then further, He was the silent Lamb. 'As a sheep before her shearers is dumb, so he openeth not his mouth.' Facing the calumnies of men, we read, 'He answered nothing.' He never defended Himself, nor explained Himself. But we have been anything but silent when others have said unkind or untrue things about us. Our voices have been loud in self-defence and self-vindication, and there has been anger in our voices. We have excused ourselves when we should have admitted frankly our wrong. On every such occasion the Dove had to take His flight and withdraw His peace and blessing from our hearts, because we were not willing to be the silent lamb.

No Grudges

He was also the spotless Lamb. Not only did nothing escape His lips, but there was nothing in His heart but

love for those who had sent Him to the Cross. There was
no resentment towards them, no grudges, no bitterness.
Even as they were putting the nails through His hands,
He was murmuring, 'I forgive you,' and He asked His
Father to forgive them too. He was willing to suffer it in
meekness for us. But what resentment and bitterness have
not we had in our hearts—toward this one and that one,
and over so much less than what they did to Jesus. Each
reaction left a stain on our hearts, and the Dove had to fly
away because we were not willing to bear it and forgive
it for Jesus' sake.

Return, O Dove!

These, then, are the acts and attitudes which drive the
Holy Spirit from our lives, as far as present blessing is
concerned, and they are all sin. Sin is the only thing that
hinders the revival of His Church. The question of all
questions for us just now is, 'How can the Dove return
to our lives with His grace and power?' The answer is
again just simply, 'The Lamb of God', for He is not only
the simple Lamb and the shorn Lamb and the silent Lamb
and the spotless Lamb, but above everything else He is
the substitute Lamb.

To the Jew, the lamb that was offered to God was always
a substitute lamb. Its meekness and submissiveness were
only incidental to its main work, that of being slain for
his sin and of having its blood sprinkled on the altar to
atone for it. The humility of the Lord Jesus in becoming
our Lamb was necessary only that on the Cross He might
become our Substitute, our scapegoat, carrying our sins
in His own Body on the Tree, so that there might be
forgiveness for our sins and cleansing from all their stains,

when we repent of them. God wants, moreover, to take us back to that Cross and show us our sins wounding and hurting the Lamb. 'Were you there when they crucified my Lord?' asks the old negro spiritual.

The answer is, 'Yes, we were.' By our unwillingness to 'break', we show that we were part of that crowd slaying Him at Calvary. And our gentle Lamb was willing for them and us to do it, in order that, when at last we repent, there might be precious Blood to secure our forgiveness and to cleanse us from all sin. May this solemn thought break our proud hearts in repentance! For it is only when we have seen these sins of ours in the heart of Jesus, so that we are broken and willing to repent of them and put them right, that the Blood of the Lamb cleanses us from them and the Dove returns with peace and blessing to our hearts.

He humbled Himself to the manger,
And even to Calvary's tree;
But I am so proud and unwilling,
His humble disciple to be.

He yielded His will to the Father,
And chose to abide in the Light;
But I prefer wrestling to resting,
And try by myself to do right.

Lord break me, then cleanse me and fill me
And keep me abiding in Thee;
That fellowship may be unbroken,
And Thy Name be hallowed in me.

A saintly African Christian once told a congregation that as he was climbing the hill to the meeting he heard steps behind him. He turned and saw a man carrying a very heavy load up the hill on his back. He was full of sympathy for him and spoke to him. Then he noticed that His hands were scarred, and he realized that it was Jesus. He said to Him, 'Lord, are you carrying the world's sin up the hill?' 'No,' said the Lord Jesus, 'not the world's sin, just yours!' As that African simply told the vision God had just given him, the people's hearts and his heart were broken as they saw their sins at the Cross. Our hearts need to be broken too, and only when they are, shall we be willing for the confessions, the apologies, the reconciliations, and the restitutions that are involved in a true repentance of sin. Then, when we have been willing to humble ourselves, as the Lord humbled Himself, the Dove will return to us.

> Return, O heavenly Dove, return,
> Sweet messenger of rest!
> I hate the sins that made Thee mourn,
> And drove Thee from my breast.

Ruled by the Dove

One last word. The Dove is the emblem of peace, which suggests that if the Blood of Jesus has cleansed us and we are walking with the Lamb in humility, the sign of the Spirit's presence and fullness will be peace. This is indeed to be the test of our walk all the way along. 'Let the peace of God rule [or arbitrate] in your hearts.'[10] If the Dove ceases to sing in our hearts at any time, if our peace is

---

[10] Col. 3:15

broken, then it can be only because of sin. In some matter we have departed from the humility of the Lamb. We must ask God to show us what it is, and be quick to repent of it and bring the sin to the Cross. Then the Dove will be once again in His rightful place in our hearts, and peace with God will be ours. In this way we shall know that continuous abiding of the Spirit's presence which is open even to fallen men through the immediate and constant application of the precious Blood of Jesus.

Shall we not begin from today to allow our lives to be ruled by the Heavenly Dove, the peace of God, and allow Him to be the arbiter all the day through? We shall find ourselves walking in a path of constant conviction and much humbling, but in this way we shall come into real conformity with the Lamb of God, and we shall know the only victory that is worth anything, the conquest of self.

6

Revival in the Home

Thousands of years ago, in the most beautiful Garden the world has ever known, lived a man and a woman. Formed in the likeness of their Creator, they lived solely to reveal Him to His creation and to each other, and thus to glorify Him every moment of the day. Humbly they accepted the position of a creature with the Creator— that of complete submission and yieldedness to His will. Because they always submitted their wills to His, because they lived for Him and not for themselves, they were also completely submitted to each other. Thus in that first home in that beautiful garden there was absolute harmony, peace, love, and oneness, not only with God but also with each other.

Then one day the harmony was shattered, for the serpent stole into that God-centred home, and with him, sin. And now, because they had lost their peace and fellowship with God, they lost it with each other. No longer did they live for God—they each lived for themselves. They were each their own gods now, and because they no longer lived for God, they no longer lived for each other. Instead of peace, harmony, love, and oneness, there was now discord and hate—in other words, SIN!

Revival Begins at Home

It was into the home that sin first came. It is in the home that we sin more than perhaps anywhere else, and it is to the home that revival first needs to come. Revival is desperately needed in the Church, in the country, and in the world, but a revived Church with unrevived homes would be sheer hypocrisy. It is the hardest place, the most costly, but the most necessary place to begin.

Before we go on, however, let us remind ourselves again of what revival really is. It simply means new life in hearts where the spiritual life has ebbed—but not a new life of self-effort or self-initiated activity. It is not man's life, but God's Life, the Life of Jesus filling us and flowing through us. That Life is manifested in fellowship and oneness with those with whom we live—nothing between us and God, and nothing between us and others. The home is the place before all others where this should be experienced.

How different is the experience of so many of us professing Christians in our homes—little irritations, frayed tempers, selfishness, and resentments; and even where there is nothing very definitely wrong between us, just not that complete oneness and fellowship that ought to characterize Christians living together. All the things that come between us and others, come between us and God, and spoil our fellowship with Him, so that our hearts are not overflowing with the Divine Life.

What is Wrong with our Homes?

Now what at bottom is wrong with our homes? When we talk about homes we mean the relationship which exists beween a husband and wife, a parent and child, a brother and sister, or between any others who, through various circumstances, are compelled to live together.

The first thing that is wrong with so many families is that they are not really open with one another. We live so largely behind drawn blinds. The others do not know us for what we really are, and we do not intend that they should. Even those living in the most intimate relationships with us do not know what goes on inside—our difficulties, battles, failures, nor what the Lord Jesus has to cleanse us from so frequently. This lack of transparency and openness is ever the result of sin. The first effect of the first sin was to make Adam and Eve hide from God behind the trees of the Garden. They who had been so transparent with God and with one another were then hiding from God because of sin; and if they hid from God you can be quite sure that they soon began to hide from one another. There were reactions and thoughts in Adam's heart that Eve was never allowed to know, and there were like things hidden in Eve's heart too. So it has been ever since. Having something to hide from God, we hide it, too, from one another. Behind that wall of reserve, which acts like a mask, we cover our real selves. Sometimes we hide in the most extraordinary way behind an assumed jocular manner. We are afraid to be serious because we do not want others to get too close and see us as we really are, and so we keep up a game of bluff. We are not real with one another, and no one can have fellowship with an unreal person, and so oneness and close fellowship are impossible in the home. This is what the Scripture calls 'walking in darkness'—for the darkness is anything which hides.

The Failure to Love

The second thing that is wrong with our homes is our failure really to love one another. 'Well,' says somebody, 'that could never be said of our home, for no one could love one another more than my husband and I love each other!' But wait a minute! It depends on what you mean by love. Love is not just a sentimental feeling, nor even strong passion. The famous passage in 1 Cor. 13 tells us what real love is, and if we test ourselves by it we may find that, after all, we are hardly loving one another at all, and our behaviour is all in the opposite direction—and the opposite of love is hate! Let us look at some of the things that that passage tells us about love.

> 'Love suffereth long *(is patient)*
>   and is kind;
> love envieth not *(is not jealous)*;
> love vaunteth not itself *(does not boast)*,
>   is not puffed up *(is not conceited)*,
>   doth not behave itself unseemly *(is not rude)*,
>   seeketh not her own *(is not selfish)*,
>   is not easily provoked *(does not get irritated)*,
>   thinketh no evil *(does not entertain unkind thoughts of another)*.'

How do we stand up to these tests in our homes? So often we act in the very opposite way.

We are often impatient with one another and even unkind in the way we answer back or react.

How much jealousy, too, there can be in a home. A husband and wife can be jealous of one another's gifts, even of their spiritual progress. Parents may be jealous of their children, and how often is there not bitter jealousy between brothers and sisters.

Also 'not behaving unseemly', that is, courtesy: what about that? Courtesy is just love in little things, but it is in the little things that we trip up. We think we can 'let up' at home.

How 'puffed up', that is, conceited, we so often are! Conceit comes out in all sorts of ways. We think we know best. We want our way, and we nag or boss the other one, and nagging or bossing leads on to the tendency to despise the other one. Our very attitude of superiority sets us up above them. Then, when at the bottom of our hearts we despise someone, we blame them for everything—and yet we think we love.

Then what about 'seeking not our own', that is, not being selfish? Many times a day we put our wishes and interests before those of the other one.

How 'easily provoked' we are! How quick to be irritated by something in the other! How often we allow the unkind thought, the resentful feeling over something the other has done or left undone! Yet we profess there are no failures in love in our homes. These things happen every day, and we think nothing of them. They are all of them the opposite of love, and the opposite of love is hate. Impatience is hate. Envy is hate. Conceit and self-will are hate, and so are selfishness, irritability, and resentment! And hate is SIN. 'He that saith he is in the light, and hateth his brother, is in darkness even until now.'[11] What tensions, barriers, and discord it all causes,

---

[11] 1 John 2:9

and fellowship with God and the other person is made impossible.

The Only Way Out

Now the question is, 'Do I want new life, revival, in my home?' I have got to challenge my heart about this. Am I prepared to continue in this state, or am I really hungry for new life, His life, in my home? For not unless I am really hungry will I be willing to take the necessary steps. The first step I must take is to call sin, sin (my sin, not the other person's) and go with it to the Cross, and trust the Lord Jesus there and then to cleanse me from it.

As we bow the neck at the Cross, His self-forgetful love for the others, His longsuffering and forbearance flow into our hearts. The precious Blood cleanses us from the 'unlove' and illwill, and the Holy Spirit fills us with the very nature of Jesus. 1 Cor. 13 is nothing less than the nature of Jesus, and it is all a gift to us, for His nature is ours, if He is ours. This blessed process can happen every single time the beginning of sin and unlove creep in, for the cleansing fountain of Blood is available for us all the time.

All this will commit us very definitely to walking the Way of the Cross in our homes. Again and again we will see places where we must yield up our rights, as Jesus yielded up His for us. We shall have to see that the thing in us that reacts so sharply to another's selfishness and pride is simply our own selfishness and pride, which we are unwilling to sacrifice. We shall have to accept another's ways and doings as God's will for us and meekly bend the neck to all God's providences. That does not mean that we must accept another's selfishness as God's will for

them—far from it—but only as God's will for us. As far as
the other is concerned, God will probably want to use us,
if we are broken, to help him see his need. Certainly, if we
are a parent we shall often need to correct our child with
firmness. But none of this is to be from selfish motives,
but only out of love for the other and a longing for their
good. Our own convenience and rights must all the time
be yielded. Only thus will the love of the Lord Jesus be
able to fill us and express itself through us.

When we have been broken at Calvary we must be
willing to put things right with the others—sometimes
even with the children. This is, so often, the test of our
brokenness. Brokenness is the opposite of hardness.
Hardness says, 'It's your fault!' Brokenness, however,
says, 'It's my fault!' What a different atmosphere will
begin to prevail in our homes when they hear us say that!
Let us remember that at the Cross there is only room for
one at a time. We cannot say, 'I was wrong, but you were
wrong too. You must come as well!' No, you must go
alone, saying, 'I'm wrong.' God will work in the other
more through your brokenness than through anything else
you can do or say. We may, however, have to wait perhaps
a long time. But that should only cause us to understand
more perfectly how God feels, for, as someone has said,
'He, too, has had to wait a long time since His great
attempt to put things right with man nineteen hundred
years ago, although there was no wrong on His side.' But
God will surely answer our prayer and bring the other to
Calvary too. There we shall be one; there the middle wall
of partition between us will be broken down; there we
shall be able to walk in the light, in true transparency with

Jesus and with one another, loving each other with a pure heart fervently. Sin is almost the only thing we have in common with everyone else, and so at the feet of Jesus, where sin is cleansed, is the only place where we can be one. Real oneness conjures up for us the picture of two or more sinners together at Calvary.

7

The Mote and the Beam

That friend of ours has got something in his eye! Though it is only something tiny—what Jesus called a mote—how painful it is, and how helpless he is until it is removed! It is surely our part as a friend to do all we can to remove it, and how grateful he is to us when we have succeeded in doing so. We should be equally grateful to him, if he did the same service for us.

In the light of that, it seems clear that the real point of the well-known passage in Matt. 7:3–5 about the beam and the mote is not the forbidding of our trying to remove the fault in the other person, but rather the reverse. It is the injunction that at all costs we should do this service for one another. True, its first emphasis seems to be a condemnation of censoriousness, but when the censoriousness in us is removed, the passage ends by saying, 'Then shalt thou see clearly to cast out the mote out of thy brother's eye.' According to the New Testament, we are meant to care so much for the other man, that we are willing to do all we can to remove from his eye the mote which is marring his vision and hindering his blessing. We are told to 'admonish one another' and 'exhort one another', to 'wash one another's feet' and 'to provoke one another to love and good works'. The love of Jesus poured out in us will make us want to help our brother in this way.

What blessing may not come to many others through our willingness humbly to challenge one another, as led by God. A humble Swiss, named Nicholas of Basle, one of the Society of the Friends of God, crossed the mountains to Strasburg and entered the Church of Dr. Tauler, the popular preacher of that city. Said Nicholas, 'Dr. Tauler, before you can do your greatest work for God, the world, and this city, you must die—die to yourself, your gifts, your popularity, and even your own goodness, and when you have learned the full meaning of the Cross, you will have a new power with God and man.' That humble challenge from an obscure Christian changed Dr. Tauler's life, and he did indeed learn to die, and became one of the great factors to prepare the way for Luther and the Reformation. In this passage the Lord Jesus tells us how we may do this service for one another.

What is the Beam?

First, however, the Lord Jesus tells us that it is only too possible to try to take the tiny mote, a tiny speck of sawdust, out of the other's eye when there is a beam, a great length of timber, in our own. When that is the case we haven't a chance of casting out the mote in the other, because we cannot see straight ourselves, and in any case it is sheer hypocrisy to attempt to do so.

Now we all know what Jesus meant by the mote in the other person's eye. It is some fault which we fancy we can discern in him; it may be an act he has done against us, or some attitude he adopts towards us. But what did the Lord Jesus mean by the beam in our eye? I suggest that the beam in our eye is simply our unloving reaction to

the other man's mote. Without doubt there is a wrong in
the other person, but our reaction to that wrong is wrong
too! The mote in him has provoked in us resentment, or
coldness, or criticism, or bitterness, or evil speaking, or
ill-will—all of them variants of the basic ill, unlove. And
that, says the Lord Jesus, is far, far worse than the tiny
wrong (sometimes quite unconscious) that provoked it. In
the Greek a mote means a little splinter, whereas a beam
means a rafter. By this comparison the Lord Jesus means
to tell us that our unloving reaction to the other's wrong
is what a great rafter is to a little splinter! Every time
we point one of our fingers at another and say, 'It's your
fault', three of our fingers are pointing back at us. God
have mercy on us for the many times when it has been so
with us and in our hypocrisy we have tried to deal with the
other person's fault, when God saw there was this thing
far worse in our own hearts.

But let us not think that a beam is of necessity some
violent reaction on our part. The first beginning of a
resentment is a beam, as is also the first flicker of an unkind
thought, or the first suggestion of unloving criticism.
Where that is so, it only distorts our vision, and we shall
never see our brother as he really is, beloved of God. If
we speak to our brother with that in our hearts, it will only
provoke him to adopt the same hard attitude to us, for it is
a law of human relationships that 'with what measure ye
mete, it shall be measured to you again.'[12]

Take it to Calvary

No! 'First cast out the beam out of thine own eye.' That is
the first thing we must do. We must recognize our unloving

[12] Matt. 7:2

reaction to him as sin. On our knees we must go with it to Calvary, see Jesus there, and get a glimpse of what that sin cost Him. At His Feet we must repent of it, and be broken afresh, and trust the Lord Jesus to cleanse it away in His precious Blood and fill us with His love for that one—and He will, and does, if we will claim His promise. Then we shall probably need to go to the other in the attitude of the repentant one, tell him of the sin that has been in our heart and what the Blood has effected there, and ask him to forgive us too. Very often bystanders will tell us, and sometimes our own hearts, that the sin we are confessing is not nearly so bad as the other's wrong, which he is not yet confessing. But we have been to Calvary, indeed we are learning to live under the shadow of Calvary, and we have seen our sin there and we can no longer compare our sin with another's.

As we take these simple steps of repentance, then we can see clearly to cast the mote out of the other's eye, for the beam in our eye has gone. In that moment God will pour light in on us as to the other's need, that neither he nor we ever had before. We may see then that the mote we were so conscious of before is virtually non-existent—it was but the projection of something that was in us. On the other hand, we may have revealed to us hidden, under-lying things, of which he himself was hardly conscious. Then, as God leads us, we must lovingly and humbly challenge him, so that he may see them too, and bring them to the Fountain for sin and find deliverance. He will be more likely than ever to let us do it—indeed, if he is a humble man he will be grateful to us, for he will know now that there is no selfish motive in our heart, but only love and concern for him.

When God is leading us to challenge another, let not fear hold us back. Let us not argue or press our point. Let us just say what God has told us to and leave it there. It is God's work, not ours, to cause the other to see it. It takes time to be willing to bend 'the proud, stiff-necked I'. When we in turn are challenged, let us not defend ourselves and explain ourselves. Let us take it in silence, thanking the other; and then go to God about it and ask Him. If he was right, let us be humble enough to go and tell him, and praise God together. There is no doubt that we need each other desperately. There are blind spots in all our lives that we shall never see, unless we are prepared for another to be God's channel to us.

8

Are you Willing to be a Servant?

Nothing is clearer from the New Testament than that the Lord Jesus expects us to take the low position of servants. This is not just an extra obligation which we may or may not assume as we please. It is the very heart of that new relationship which the disciple is to take up to God and to his fellows if he is to know fellowship with Christ and any degree of holiness in his life. When we understand the humbling and self-emptying that is involved in really being a servant, it becomes evident that only those who are prepared to live quite definitely under the shadow of Calvary, ever contemplating the humility and brokenness of the Lord Jesus for us, will be willing for that position.

As we approach this subject and its personal application in detail to our lives, there are three preliminary things which need to be said to prepare us to understand the low and humbling position which He wants us to take.

In the Old Testament two sorts of servants are mentioned. There are the hired servants, who have wages paid to them and have certain rights. Then there are the bond-servants, or slaves, who have no rights, who receive no wages, and who have no appeal. The Hebrews were forbidden ever to make bond-servants of their own race. Only of the Gentiles were they permitted to take such slaves. When, however, we come to the New Testament, the word in the Greek for the servant of the Lord Jesus Christ is not 'hired servant' but 'bond-servant', by which is meant to be shown that our position is one where we have no rights and no appeal, where we are the absolute property of our Master, to be treated and disposed of just as He wishes.

Further, we shall see more clearly still what our position is to be when we understand that we are to be the bond-servants of One who was Himself willing to be a bond-servant. Nothing shows better the amazing humility of the Lord Jesus, whose servants we are to be, than that though He was 'in the form of God', He 'counted it not a prize to be on an equality with God, but emptied himself, taking the form of a servant'[13]—without rights, willing to be treated as the will of the Father and the malice of men might decree, if only He might thereby serve men and bring them back to God. And you and I are to be the bond-servants of Him who was and always is a bond-servant, whose disposition is ever that of humility and whose activity is ever that of humbling Himself to serve His creatures. How utterly low, then, is our true position! How this shows us what it means to be ruled by the Lord Jesus!

That leads us to something further. Our servanthood to the Lord Jesus is to express itself in our servanthood to our fellows. Says Paul, 'We preach not ourselves, but Christ Jesus the Lord; and ourselves your servants for Jesus' sake.'[14] The low position we take toward the Lord Jesus is judged by Him by the low position we take in

---

[13] Phil. 2:6-7 (RV)   [14] 2 Cor. 4:5

our relationship with our fellows. An unwillingness to serve others in costly, humbling ways He takes to be an unwillingness to serve Him, and we thus put ourselves out of fellowship with Him.

We are now in a position to apply all this much more personally to our lives. God spoke to me some time ago through Luke 17:7–10. 'But which of you having a servant plowing or feeding cattle, will say unto him by and by, when he is come from the field, Go and sit down to meat? And will not rather say unto him, Make ready wherewith I may sup, and gird thyself, and serve me, till I have eaten and drunken; and afterward thou shalt eat and drink? Doth he thank that servant because he did the things that were commanded him? I trow not. So likewise ye, when ye shall have done all those things which are commanded you, say, We are unprofitable servants: we have done that which was our duty to do.'

I see here five marks of the bond-servant. First of all, he must be willing to have one thing on top of another put upon him, without any consideration being given him. On top of a hard day in the field the servant in the parable had immediately to prepare his master's meal, and on top of that he had to wait at table—and all that before he had any food himself. He just went and did it, expecting nothing else. How unwilling we are for this! How quickly there are murmurings and bitterness in our hearts when that sort of thing is expected of us. But the moment we start murmuring, we are acting as if we had rights, and a bond-servant hasn't any!

Secondly, in doing this he must be willing not to be thanked for it. How often we serve others, but what self-

pity we have in our hearts and how bitterly we complain
that they take it as a matter of course and do not thank us
for it. But a bond-servant must be willing for that. Hired
servants may expect something, but not bond-servants.

And, thirdly, having done all this, he must not charge
the other with selfishness. As I read the passage, I
could not but feel that the master was rather selfish and
inconsiderate, but there is no such charge from the bond-
servant. He exists to serve the interests of his master, and
the selfishness or otherwise of his master does not come
into it with him. But we? We can perhaps allow ourselves
to be 'put upon' by others, and are willing, perhaps, not to
be thanked for what we do, yet how we charge the other
in our minds with selfishness! But that is not the place of a
bond-servant. He is to find in the selfishness of others but
a further opportunity to identify himself afresh with His
Lord as the servant of all.

There is, however, a fourth step still to which we must
go. Having done all that, there is no ground for pride
or self-congratulation, but we must confess that we are
unprofitable servants, that is, that we are of no real use
to God or man in ourselves. We must confess again and
again that 'in me (that is, in my flesh), dwelleth no good
thing',[15] that, if we have acted thus, it is no thanks to us,
whose hearts are naturally proud and stubborn, but only
to the Lord Jesus, who dwells in us and who has made us
willing.

The bottom of self is quite knocked out by the fifth and
last step—the admission that doing and bearing what we
have in the way of meekness and humility, we have not

[15] Rom. 7:18

done one stitch more than it was our duty to do. God made man in the first place simply that he might be God's bond-servant. Man's sin has simply consisted in his refusal to be God's bond-servant. His restoration can be, then, only a restoration to the position of a bond-servant. Man, then, has not done anything specially meritorious when he has consented to take that position, for he was created and redeemed for that very thing.

This, then, is the way of the Cross. It is the way that God's lowly Bond-servant first trod for us, and should not we, the bond-servants of that Bondservant, tread it still? Does it seem hard and forbidding, this way down? Be assured, it is the only way up. It was the way by which the Lord Jesus reached the Throne, and it is the way by which we, too, reach the place of spiritual power, authority, and fruitfulness. Those who tread this path are radiant, happy souls, overflowing with the life of their Lord. They have found 'he that humbleth himself shall be exalted'[16] to be true for them as for their Lord. Where before humility was an unwelcome intruder to be put up with only on occasions, she has now become the spouse of their souls, to whom they have wedded themselves for ever. If darkness and unrest enter their souls it is only because somewhere on some point they have been unwilling to walk with her in the paths of meekness and brokenness. But she is ever ready to welcome them back into her company, as they seek her face in repentance.

That brings us to the all-important matter of repentance. We shall not enter into more abundant life merely by resolving that we shall be humbler in the future. There are

---

[16] Luke 14:11

attitudes and actions which have already taken place and are still being persisted in (if only by our unwillingness to apologize for them) that must first be repented of. The Lord Jesus did not take upon Him the form of a bond-servant merely to give us an example, but that He might die for these very sins upon the Cross, and open a fountain in His precious Blood where they can all be washed away. That Blood, however, cannot be applied to the sins of our proud hearts until we have been broken in repentance over what has already happened and over what we already are. This will mean allowing the light of God to go through every part of our hearts and into every part of our relationships. It will mean that we shall have to see that the sins of pride, which God will show us, made it necessary for Jesus to come from heaven and die on the Cross that they might be forgiven. It will mean not only asking Him to forgive us but asking others too. That will be humbling indeed. But as we crawl through the door of the broken ones, we shall emerge into the light and glory of the highway of holiness and humility.

9

The Power of the Blood of the Lamb

The message and challenge of revival which is coming to many of us these days is searching in its utter simplicity. It is simply that there is only one thing in the world that can hinder the Christian's walking in victorious fellowship with God and his being filled with the Holy Spirit—and that is sin in one form or another. There is only one thing in the world that can cleanse him from sin, with all that means of liberty and victory—and that is the power of the Blood of the Lord Jesus. It is, however, most important for us that we should see what it is that gives the Blood of Christ its mighty power with God on behalf of men, for then we shall understand the conditions on which its full power may be experienced in our lives.

How many achievements and how many blessings for men the Scripture ascribes to the power of the Blood of the Lord Jesus! By the power of His Blood peace is made between man and God.[17] By its power there is forgiveness of sins and eternal life for all who put their faith in the Lord Jesus.[18] By the power of His Blood Satan is overcome.[19] By its power there is continual cleansing from all sin for us.[20] By the power of His Blood we may be set free

---

[17] Col. 1:20   [18] Col. 1:14; John 6:54   [19] Rev. 12:11   [20] 1 John 1:7

from the tyranny of an evil conscience to serve the living God.[21] By its infinite power with God the most unworthy have liberty to enter the Holy of Holies of God's presence and live there all the day.[22] We may well ask what gives the Blood its power!

To that question we need to link this other question—how may we experience its full power in our lives? Too often that precious Blood does not have its sin-cleansing, peace-giving, life-imparting power in our hearts, and too often we do not find ourselves in God's presence and fellowship all the day.

Whence its Power?

The answer to the first question is suggested by the phrase in the book of Revelation which describes the Blood of Christ by the tender expression, 'the blood of the Lamb'.[23] Not the Blood of the Warrior, but the Blood of *the Lamb*! In other words, that which gives the precious Blood its power with God for men is the lamb-like disposition of the One who shed it, and of which it is the supreme expression. The title 'the Lamb', so frequently given to the Lord Jesus in Scripture, is first of all descriptive of His work—that of being a sacrifice for our sin. When a sinning Israelite wanted to get right with God, it was the blood of a lamb (sometimes that of a goat) which had to be shed and sprinkled on the altar. Jesus is the Divine fulfilment of all those lambs that men offered—the Lamb of God, which taketh away the sin of the world.[24] But the title 'the Lamb' has a deeper meaning. It describes His character. He is the Lamb in that He is meek and lowly in heart,[25] gentle and un-

---

[21] Heb. 9:14 [22] Heb. 10:19 [23] Rev. 7:14 [24] John 1:29 [25] Matt. 11:29

resisting, and all the time surrendering His own will to the Father's[26] for the blessing and saving of men. Anyone but the Lamb would have resented and resisted the treatment men gave Him, but He, in obedience to the Father,[27] and out of love for us, did neither. Men did what they liked to Him, and for our sakes He yielded all the time. When He was reviled, He reviled not again. When He suffered, He threatened not. No standing up for His rights, no hitting back, no resentment, no complaining! How different from us! When the Father's will and the malice of men pointed to dark Calvary, the Lamb meekly bowed His head in willingness for that too. It was as the Lamb that Isaiah saw Him, when he prophesied, 'He is brought as a lamb to the slaughter, and as a sheep before her shearers is dumb, so he openeth not his mouth.'[28] The scourging, the scoffing, the spitting, the hair plucked from His cheeks, the weary last march up the Hill, the nailing and the lifting up, the piercing of His side and the flowing of His Blood—none of these things would ever have been, had He not been the Lamb. And all that to pay the price of *my* sin! So we see that He is not merely the Lamb because He died on the Cross, but He died upon the Cross because He is the Lamb.

Let us ever see this disposition in the Blood. Let every mention of the Blood call to mind the deep humility and self-surrender of the Lamb, for it is this disposition that gives the Blood its wonderful power with God. Heb. 9:14 for ever links the Blood of Christ with His self-offering to God, 'how much more shall the blood of Christ, who through the eternal Spirit *offered himself* without spot to God....'[29] And

---

[26] John 6:38   [27] Phil.2:8   [28] Is. 53:7   [29] Heb. 9:14

it is this fact that bestows upon it its power with God for men, for this disposition has ever been of supreme value to God. Humility, lamb-likeness, the surrender of our wills to God are what He looks for supremely from man. It was to manifest all this that God ever created the first man. It was his refusal to walk this path that constituted his first sin, and it has been the heart of sin ever since. It was to bring this disposition back to earth that Jesus came. It was simply because the Father saw this in Him that He could say, 'This is my beloved Son, in whom I am well pleased.'[29] It was because the shedding of His Blood so supremely expressed this disposition that it is so utterly precious to God and so all-availing for man and his sin.

The Second Question

We come now to the second question—how can we experience its full power in our lives? Our hearts surely tell us the answer, as we look on the Lamb, bowing His Head for us on Calvary—only by being willing to have the same disposition that ruled Him and by bending our necks in brokenness as He bowed His. Just as it is the disposition of the Lamb that bestows upon the Blood its power, so it is only as we are willing to be partakers of the same disposition of the Lamb, that we shall know its full power in our lives. And we *can* be partakers of His disposition,[31] for it has been made transferable to us by His death. All the fruits of the Holy Spirit, mentioned in Gal. 5—love, joy, peace, long-suffering, gentleness, goodness, faith, meekness, self-control—what are they but the expressions of the lamb-like nature of the Lord Jesus, with which the

---

[30] Matt. 3:17   [31] Phil. 2:5; 1 Cor. 2:16

Holy Spirit wants to fill us? Let us never forget that the Lord Jesus, though exalted to the throne of God, is still the Lamb (the book of Revelation tells us that) and He wants to reproduce Himself in us.

Are We Willing?

But are we willing for this? There is a hard, unyielding self, which stands up for itself and resists others, that will have to be broken, if we are to be willing for the disposition of the Lamb, and if the precious Blood is to reach us in cleansing power. We may pray long to be cleansed from some sin and for peace to be restored to our hearts, but unless we are willing to be broken on the point in question and be made partakers of the Lamb's humility there, nothing will happen. Every sin we ever commit is the result of the hard, unbroken self taking up some attitude of pride, and we shall not find peace through the Blood until we are willing to see the source of each sin, and reverse the wrong attitude that caused it by a specific repentance, which will always be humbling. This means that we have not merely to try to make ourselves feel the humility of Jesus. We have only to walk in the light and be willing for God to reveal any sin that may be in our lives, and we shall find ourselves asked by the Lord to perform all sorts of costly acts of repentance and surrender, often over what we term small and trivial matters. Their importance, however, can be gauged by what it costs our pride to put them right. He may show us a confession or apology that has to be made to someone or an act of restitution that has to be done.[32] He may show us that we must climb down over

---

[32] Matt. 5:23-24

something and yield up our fancied rights in it (Jesus had
no rights—have we then?). He may show us that we must
go to the one who has done a wrong and confess to him
the far greater wrong of resenting it (Jesus never resented
anything or anyone—have we any right to?). He may call
us to be open with our friends that they may know us as
we really are, and thus be able to have true fellowship
with us. These acts may be humiliating and a complete
reversal of our usual attitudes of pride and selfishness, but
by such acts we shall know true brokenness and become
partakers of the humility of the Lamb. As we are willing
for this in each issue, the Blood of the Lamb will be able
to cleanse us from all sin, and we shall walk with God in
white, with His peace in our hearts.

10

Protesting Our Innocence?

We have all become so used to condemning the proud, self-righteous attitude of the Pharisee in the parable of the Pharisee and the Publican,[33] that we can hardly believe that the picture of him there is meant to apply to us—which only shows how much like him we really are. The Sunday-school teacher was never so much a Pharisee as when she finished her lesson on this parable with the words, 'And now, children, we can thank God that we are not as this Pharisee!' In particular are we in danger of adopting the Pharisee's attitude when God is wanting to humble us at the Cross of Jesus, and show us the sins in our hearts that are hindering personal revival.

God's Picture of the Human Heart

We shall not understand the real wrong of the Pharisee's attitude, nor of our own, unless we view it against the background of what God says about the human heart. Said Jesus Christ, 'From within, out of the heart of men, proceed evil thoughts, adulteries, fornications, murders, thefts, covetousness, wickedness, deceit, lasciviousness, an evil eye, blasphemy, pride, foolishness.'[34] The same

[33] Luke 18:9-14   [34] Mark 7:20-23

dark picture of the human heart is given us in Paul's letter
to the Galatians, 'The works of the flesh are manifest,
which are these: adultery, fornication, uncleanness,
lasciviousness, idolatry, witchcraft, hatred, variance,
emulations, wrath, strife, seditious, heresies, envyings,
murders, drunkenness, revellings, and such like.'[35] What
a picture! Jeremiah adds the same witness, 'The heart
is deceitful above all things [that is, it deceives the man
himself, so that he does not know himself], and desperately
wicked : who can know it?'[36] Here, then, is God's picture
of the human heart, the fallen self, 'the old man,'[37] as the
Scripture calls it, whether it be in the unconverted or in
the keenest Christian. It is hard to believe that these things
can proceed from the heart of ministers, evangelists,
and Christian workers, but it is true. The simple truth is
that the only beautiful thing about the Christian is Jesus
Christ. God wants us to recognize that fact as true in our
experience, so that in true brokenness and self-despair
we shall allow Jesus Christ to be our righteousness and
holiness and all in all—and that is victory.

Making God a Liar!

Now in face of God's description of the human heart we
can see what it was that the Pharisee did. In saying, 'I
thank thee, that I am not as other men are, extortioners,
unjust, adulterers,' he was protesting his innocence of the
very things that God says are in every heart. He said in
effect, 'These things are doubtless true of other men—this
Publican is even now confessing them—but, Lord, not of
me!' And in so saying, he was making God a liar, for 'if we

---

[35] Gal. 5:19-21   [36] Jer. 17:9   [37] Eph. 4:22

say that we have not sinned, we make him a liar,'[38] because He says we have! Yet I feel sure that he was perfectly sincere in what he said. He really did believe that he was innocent of these things. Indeed, he is ascribing his imagined innocence to God, saying, 'I thank Thee....' God's Word, however, still stood against him, but he just had not seen it. The 'penny had not dropped'! If the Publican is beating upon his breast and confessing his sins, it is not because he has sinned worse than the Pharisee. It is simply that the Publican has seen that what God says is woefully true of him, and the Pharisee has not. The Pharisee still thinks that outward abstinence from certain sins is all that God requires. He has not yet understood that God looks, not on the outward appearance, but on the heart,[39] and accounts the look of lust the equivalent of adultery,[40] the attitude of resentment and hate the same as murder,[41] envy as actual theft, and the petty tyrannies in the home as wicked as the most extortionate dealings in the market.

How often have not we, too, protested our innocence on the many occasions when God has been convicting others, and when He has wanted to convict us too. We have said in effect, 'These things may be true of others, but not of me!' and we may have said so quite sincerely. Perhaps we have heard of others who have humbled themselves and have rather despised them for the confessions they have had to make and the things they had to put right in their lives. Or perhaps we have been genuinely glad that they have been blessed. But, whichever it is, we do not feel that we have anything to be broken about ourselves. Beloved, if we feel we are innocent and have nothing to

[38] 1 John 1:10   [39] 1 Sam. 16:7   [40] Matt. 5:27-28   [41] 1 John 3:15

be broken about, it is not that these things are not there, but that we have not seen them.

We have been living in a realm of illusion about ourselves. God must be true in all that He says about us. In one form or another He sees these things expressing themselves in us (unless we have recognized them and allowed God to deal with them)—unconscious selfishness, pride, and self-congratulation; jealousy, resentment, and impatience; reserve, fears, and shyness; dishonesty and deception; impurity and lust; if not one thing, then another. But we are blind to it. We are, perhaps, so occupied with the wrong the other man has done us, that we do not see that we are sinning against Christ in not being willing to take it with His meekness and lowliness. Seeing so clearly how the other man wants his own way and rights, we are blind to the fact that we want ours just as much; and yet we know there is something missing in our lives. Somehow we are not in vital fellowship with God. We are not spiritually crisp. Our service does not 'crackle with the supernatural'. Unconscious sin is none the less sin with God, and separates us from Him. The sin in question may be quite a small thing which God will so readily show us, if we are only willing to ask Him.

There is yet another error we fall into when we are not willing to recognize the truth of what God says of the human heart. Not only do we protest our own innocence, but we often protest the innocence of our own loved ones. We hate to see them being convicted and humbled and we hasten to defend them. We do not want them to confess anything. We are not only living in a realm of illusion about ourselves, but about them too, and we fear to have it shattered. But we are only defending them against God—making God a liar on their behalf, as we do on our own, and keeping them from entering into blessing, as we do ourselves.

Only a deep hunger for real fellowship with God will make us willing to cry to God for His all-revealing light, and to obey it when it is given.

Justifying God

That brings us to the Publican. With all that God says about the human heart in our minds, we can see that his confession of sin was simply a justifying of God, an admission that what God said of him was true. Perhaps like the Pharisee, he used not to believe that what God said about man was really true of him. But the Holy Spirit has shown him things in his life which prove God right, and he is broken. Not only does he justify God in all that he has said, but he doubtless justifies God in all the chastening judgments God has brought upon him. Nehemiah's prayer might well have been his, 'Howbeit thou art just in all that is brought upon us; for thou hast done right, but we have done wickedly.'[42]

This is ever the nature of true confession of sin, true brokenness. It is the confession that my sin is not just a mistake, a slip, a something which is really foreign to my heart ('It is not really like me to have such thoughts or do such things!'), but that it is something which reveals the real 'I'; that shows me to be the proud, rotten, unclean thing God says I am, that it really is like me to have such thoughts and do such things. It was in these terms that David confessed his sin, when he prayed, 'Against thee,

---

[42] Neh. 9:33

thee only, have I sinned, and done this evil in thy sight that thou mightest be justified when thou speakest, and be clear when thou judgest.'[43] Let us not fear, then, to make such a confession where God convicts us that we must, thinking that it will 'let Jesus down'. Rather the reverse is true, for out of such confession God gets glory, for we declare Him to be right. This brings us to a new experience of victory in Christ, for it declares afresh, that 'in me (that is, in my flesh), dwelleth no good thing,'[44] and brings us to a place where we give up trying to make our incorrigible selves holy, and where we take Jesus to be our holiness and His life to be our life.

Peace and Cleansing

But the Publican did something more than justify God. He pointed to the sacrifice on the altar, and found peace with God and cleansing from sin as he did so. That comes out in the literal meaning of the words which he uttered, 'God be merciful to me, a sinner.' In the Greek, the words mean literally, 'God be propitiated to me, the sinner.' The only way by which a Jew knew that God could be propitiated was by a sacrifice, and in all probability at that very hour the lamb for the daily burnt offering was being offered up on the altar in the temple.

With us it is the same. A man never comes to this position of brokenness but God shows him the Divine Lamb on Calvary's Cross, putting away his sins by the shedding of His Blood. The God who declares beforehand what we are, provides beforehand for our sin. Jesus was the Lamb slain for our sins from the foundation of the world. In Him,

---

[43] Psalm 51:4   [44] Rom. 7:18

who bore them in meekness, my sins are finished, and as I, in true brokenness, confess them, and put my faith in His Blood, they are cleansed and gone. Peace with God then comes into my heart, fellowship with God is immediately restored, and I walk with Him in white.

This simple way of being willing to justify God and see the power of the Blood to cleanse, brings within our reach, as never before, a close walk with Jesus, a constant dwelling with Him in the Holy of Holies. As we walk with Him in the Light, He will be showing us all the time the beginning of things, which if allowed to pass, will grieve Him and check the flow of His Life in us—things which are the expression of that old, proud self, for which God has nothing but judgment. At no point must we protest our innocence of what He shows us. All along we must be willing to justify Him and say, 'Thou art right, Lord; that just shows what I am', and be willing to give it to Him for cleansing. As we do so, we shall find that His precious Blood is continuously cleansing us from sin, so that 'the tide is being continuously healed at its beginning', and Jesus is able continuously to fill us with His Spirit. This demands that we must be men of 'a humble and contrite spirit', that is, men who are willing to be shown the smallest thing. But such are the ones, God says, who 'dwell with him in the high and holy place',[45] and who experience continuous revival.

There, then, is our choice—to protest our innocence and go down to our house, unblessed, dry of soul, and out of touch with God. Or to justify God and to enter into peace, fellowship, and victory through the Blood of Jesus.

---

[45] Is. 57:15

RHP Essential Classics

T. AUSTIN-SPARKS
  The School of Christ
  The inner working of the Holy Spirit

JOHN BUNYAN
  The Pilgrim's Progress
  The classic allegory of the Christian life

CHARLES FINNEY
  Revival
  God's way of revival

ROY HESSION
  The Calvary Road
  The way of personal revival
  We Would See Jesus
  Seeing in Jesus everything we need
  The Power of God's Grace
  The way of peace, joy and genuine revival
  When I Saw Him
  Renewing your vision of Jesus
  Our Nearest Kinsman
  The message of revival, restoration and redemption from the book of Ruth

Please ask for these titles at your local
Christian bookshop